Jul. 6, 2011

EDGE BOOKS

Build It Yourself

BUILD YOUR OWN
MINI GOLF COURSE,
LEMONADE STAND,
AND OTHER THINGS TO DO

BY TAMMY ENZ

CAPSTONE PRESS
a capstone imprint

Edge Books are published by Capstone Press,
151 Good Counsel Drive, P.O. Box 669, Mankato, Minnesota 56002.
www.capstonepub.com

 Books published by Capstone Press are manufactured with paper
containing at least 10 percent post-consumer waste.

Library of Congress Cataloging-in-Publication Data
Enz, Tammy.
    Build your own mini golf course, lemonade stand, and other
things to do / by Tammy Enz.
        p. cm.—(Edge books. Build it yourself)
    Includes bibliographical references.
    ISBN 978-1-4296-5438-8 (library binding)
    ISBN 978-1-4296-6262-8 (paperback)
1. Engineering—Juvenile literature. 2. Engineering design—Juvenile literature. 3.
Structural design—Juvenile literature. I. Title.
TA149.E586 2011
620.0078—dc22   2010032206

Editorial Credits

Aaron Sautter, editor; Ted Williams, designer; Marcy Morin, project production;
    Eric Manske, production specialist

Photo Credits

All images from Capstone Press/Karon Dubke, except:

Shutterstock/Denis and Yulia Pogostins (screws), 26, 28; DenisNata (tape measure),
    cover, 16; Dennis Steen (cork), 27; grafvision (drill bit), 14, 15; M.E. Mulder (tape),
    18, 19, 21; Morgan Lane Photography (golf ball), 8, 9; nikkytok (markers), 23, 25;
    sergwsq (paintbrush), 30; Stephanie Frey (clothespin), 24, 25; xJJx (beans), 6, 7

Design Elements/Backgrounds

Shutterstock/ARENA Creative, Eky Studio, Nanka, romvo, Vector

Capstone Press would like to thank Isaac Morin for
his help in producing the projects in this book.

Printed in the United States of America in Stevens Point, Wisconsin.
092010   005934WZS11

Table of Contents

4 Bored? Go Build Something!

BORED? GO BUILD SOMETHING!

Do you ever get bored on rainy days? Do you wish there were something awesome to do? Don't worry! Whether it's rainy or sunny, there are many cool things you can do on a lazy day.

Build a mini golf course and invite your friends over for a round of golf. Earn some money with your own lemonade stand. Imagine the fun you can have building these projects and more. All you need are a few tools and some easy-to-find materials.

Keep reading to learn how to build some simple, fun projects. Then gather your friends and get to work. Be sure to ask an adult for help when using dangerous tools. Ready to get to work? Let's go build something fun!

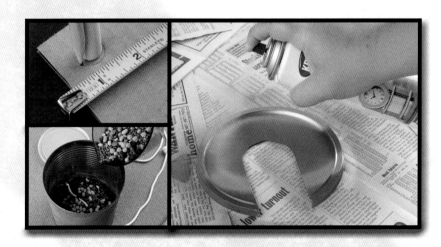

GATHER YOUR GEAR

Before you start building, take a few minutes to gather the tools listed below. Keep them organized in a toolbox so you can build your projects quickly.

MEASURING AND MARKING TOOLS

 ☐ pencil

 ☐ ruler

 ☐ tape measure

TIGHTENING AND LOOSENING TOOLS

 ☐ stapler

 ☐ screwdrivers

 ☐ hammer

 ☐ masking tape

 ☐ electrical tape

 ☐ hot glue gun

CUTTING AND SHAPING TOOLS

 ☐ drill

 ☐ rasp

 ☐ coping saw

 ☐ can openers

 ☐ metal snips

☐ scissors

 ☐ wire stripping tool

 ☐ hand saw

☐ pruning shears

 ☐ sandpaper

 ☐ utility knife

☐ wire snips

GRIPPING TOOLS

☐ needle-nose pliers

☐ pliers

5

Rattling Tin Can Stilts

Ever wish you could grow up faster? Now you can! With these rattling tin can stilts, you'll soon be towering over your friends!

 ## MATERIALS

- 2 large empty metal coffee cans with plastic lids
- dried beans or rice
- 16 feet (5 m) of rope, ¼ inch (.6 cm) thick
- paint and paintbrush

1

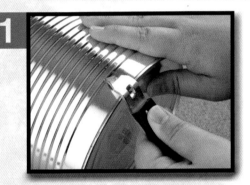

Use a puncture-style can opener to punch ¼-inch (.6-cm) holes in the coffee cans. Make the holes on opposite sides of each can, just below the bottom rim.

2

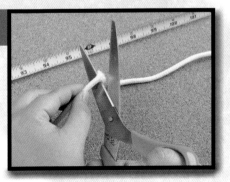

Measure and cut two 8-foot (2.5-m) pieces of rope.

3

Paint and decorate the cans any way you wish. Thread one rope through the holes of one can. Pull the two ends even and tie them together. Repeat this step with the second can.

4

Place some dried beans or rice in each can and replace the plastic lids.

5

Stand on the cans, grab the strings, and try to walk. See how much taller you are!

TIP Practice walking with your stilts on a smooth surface. Be sure to lift the cans high so you don't trip.

Mini Golf Course

You probably don't play golf like the pros. But you can still have tons of fun making your own mini golf course. Here are a few ideas to get you started. After you build these, try out some ideas of your own.

✂ MATERIALS

- plastic lids from food containers
- small cardboard boxes
- empty food containers with ends removed
- spray paint
- shoeboxes
- golf balls and clubs
- exercise hoops
- flying discs
- building blocks

1

To create the golf holes, first cut a 2-inch (5-cm) wide section from each plastic lid. The cutout sections should be U-shaped at the center of the lids. Paint each lid as you wish.

2 Cut holes on both sides of the boxes to make tunnels. Decorate the boxes and food containers any way you wish. Make enough obstacles and lids to create a nine-hole mini golf course.

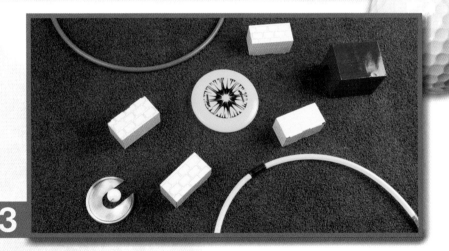

3 It's time to set up your golf course. Use the boxes, building blocks, and flying discs to create obstacles for your course. Use exercise hoops to make sand traps. Then invite your friends over to enjoy a few rounds of golf!

TIP Try using a theme for your course, such as the zoo, the farm, or outer space. Glow-in-the-dark paint can give your course a cool space glow!

Boomerang

What's better than a toy that sails high in the air and then comes back to you? Learning to use a boomerang takes some practice. But once you figure it out, there's no end to the fun!

MATERIALS

- 2 pieces of balsa wood, 12 inches (30 cm) long by 2 inches (5 cm) wide by ¼ inch (.6 cm) thick
- leather shoestring about 2 feet (.6 m) long
- spray paint

1

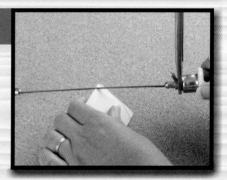

Ask an adult to help you round off all the corners of one wood piece with a coping saw.

2

Use a rasp to create a sharply angled edge along one side of the wood. The edge should extend only from the middle of the wood to the end. Rotate the wood and repeat this step on the opposite side.

Use the rasp to slightly round the remaining edges and ends of the wood.

Lightly sand the corners with sandpaper to finish rounding them. Sand the rest of the wood to make it smooth.

Paint and decorate the wood any way you wish. Repeat steps 1 to 5 with the second piece of wood.

Stack the wood pieces on top of each other in a cross shape. All the sharp edges should be facing in the same direction on the top side of the cross.

Fold the leather shoelace in half. Place it diagonally under the center of the cross. Pull the loop up over the center of the cross. Pull the ends of the shoestring through the loop.

Wrap the shoelace ends around the opposite diagonals to form an "X." Cross the ends in the back and bring them back to the front.

9

Tie the ends in a knot. Pull them as tightly as possible with two sets of pliers. Repeat this step to form a double knot.

TIP Each side of the boomerang is formed like an airplane wing. The shape helps it move and turn in the air.

10

Take the boomerang to a large outdoor area. Hold it nearly straight up and down, but turned slightly outward. Throw it like a baseball and flick your wrist as you let go. Be sure there is no danger of striking anyone with the boomerang as you throw it. With a little practice, it will zoom right back to you!

Old-Fashioned Tree Swing

Swinging under a big old shade tree is a great activity for a warm summer day. Follow the steps here to make a swing just like your grandparents may have used when they were kids.

✂ MATERIALS

- short board or piece of wood
- tree with a horizontal branch at least 6 inches (15 cm) wide
- sturdy rope, at least ½ inch (1.3 cm) thick
- ball of string
- 1 board, 2 inches (5 cm) thick by 6 inches (15 cm) wide by 18 inches (46 cm) long

1

Tie a long piece of string to the short board. Toss the board up and over the tree branch where you want your swing. Be sure to pick a branch that is strong enough to hold your weight. Let the board and string hang there for now.

2

Measure out a long piece of rope. Make it twice as long as the distance from the ground to the branch. Fold the rope in half to make a loop. Remove the string from the short board and tie it to the rope loop.

3

4

Pull on the string to pull the rope loop up and over the branch. Pull the loop down until you can reach it. Remove the string.

Slide the loose ends of the rope through the loop. Then pull on the loose ends so the loop slides back up to the branch. Pull hard to tie the rope tightly to the branch.

5

Ask an adult to help you with this step. Measure and mark 2 inches (5 cm) from each end of the long board. Be sure the marks are centered on the board. Drill a ½-inch (1.3-cm) hole through the board at these marks.

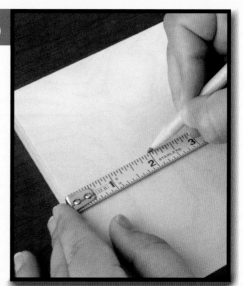

6

Thread the rope ends through the holes. Adjust the height of the swing to where you want it.

7

Tie double knots at each end of the rope on the underside of the board.

8 Trim the ropes several inches below the knots. Now hop on and enjoy your new swing!

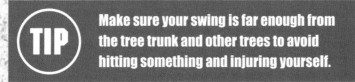

TIP Make sure your swing is far enough from the tree trunk and other trees to avoid hitting something and injuring yourself.

Kaleidoscope

Impress your friends with this homemade kaleidoscope. There's no end to the colorful patterns and designs you can make. It's easy to build and fun to share with your friends.

 MATERIALS

- empty potato chip can
- 3 clear potato chip can lids
- small, colorful beads, buttons, or other objects
- cardboard
- aluminum foil
- black permanent marker
- 1 dime
- paint and paintbrush

 1

Use a can opener to remove the metal bottom from the potato chip can.

2

Measure the length of the can. Use scissors to cut three strips of cardboard 2¼ inches (5.7 cm) wide by the length of the can. Make sure they fit snugly inside the can in the shape of a triangle.

3 Wrap each cardboard strip with foil. Be sure the shiny side of the foil faces out. Make sure the foil is kept smooth, with no wrinkles. Tape the foil in place on the back side of each strip.

4 Tape the strips into a triangle shape. Be sure the smooth, shiny sides face inward. Then slide the triangle into the can.

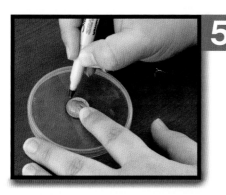

5 Use a marker to trace the shape of the dime at the center of one lid. Ask an adult to help you cut out a hole following this line with a utility knife.

6

Use the marker to color the inside of the lid black. Allow it to dry, then place the lid on top of the can.

7

Lay down a second lid with the inside facing up. Place a single layer of beads and buttons on this lid. Don't put in too many objects. Be sure there is enough room for them to move around to make different patterns.

8

Place the last lid on top of the second lid so the rims touch. Tape the lids together to form an end cap.

9

Place the bottom of the can on the end cap and tape in place. Then paint or decorate the can any way you wish.

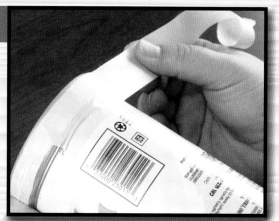

Hold the kaleidoscope up toward a light. Look through the eyehole and twist the canister to see different patterns and shapes.

10

 TIP If you have extra can lids, try making more than one end cap for the kaleidoscope. Use different kinds of colorful objects for each.

Classic Lemonade Stand

Playing on a warm summer day can make you very thirsty. Why not quench your thirst and make some money at the same time? Build this classic lemonade stand, grab a cold drink, and start making some cold, hard cash!

MATERIALS

- 4 sturdy cardboard boxes
- 1 disposable tablecloth
- 1 sheet of thick cardboard, 3 feet (.9 m) long by 3 feet wide
- 2 wooden dowels, ½ inch (1.3 cm) thick by 4 feet (1.2 m) long
- 2 empty coffee cans
- sand
- poster board
- string
- markers
- spring-loaded clothespins

1

2

Stack two boxes together on their sides. Tape them together. Repeat this step with the other two boxes.

Turn the boxes so the open sides face each other. Place them so their back sides are about 3 feet (.9 m) apart.

3

Measure and mark a line 1 foot (.3 m) from the end of one cardboard sheet. Ask an adult to help you score along this line with a utility knife.

4

Bend the cardboard at the scored line into a right angle to make a flap.

5

Place the cardboard sheet on top of the boxes so the flap hangs over the front edge. This forms the table for your stand. Secure it by taping the cardboard sheet to the boxes.

6

Ask an adult to help you slice Xs into the front corners of the table top with a utility knife. Make the Xs at the same location on each side of the table. Be sure to cut through both the cardboard sheet and the boxes.

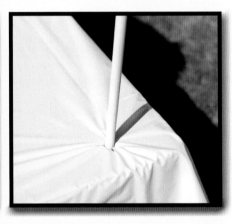

7

Place the tablecloth on the table. Tape in place on the boxes. Cut Xs in the tablecloth in the same spots as step 6. Then slide the wooden dowels through the Xs in the table top.

8

Place two coffee cans full of sand inside the boxes. Place the ends of the dowels in the cans to support them.

9

Tie string between the tops of the two dowels.

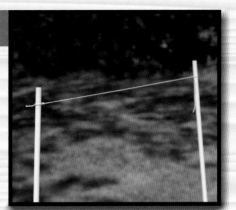

10

Cut out a sign from the poster board and decorate it with markers. Clip the sign to the dowels and the string with the clothespins. Now make some cold lemonade, sit back, and watch your money grow!

 TIP Use the inside ledges of the boxes to store your supplies and money.

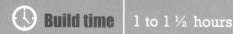

Pop Gun

This toy gun might seem dangerous, but it's not. The little cork that shoots out won't cause any damage. But the loud pop it makes will cause your friends to jump every time!

 ## MATERIALS

- 1 PVC pipe, ½ inch (1.3 cm) wide by 12 inches (30 cm) long
- 1 PVC pipe ¾ inch (1.3 cm) wide by 6 inches (15 cm) long
- 1 PVC T-connector, ¾ inch (1.9 cm) wide
- 1 screw, 1 inch (2.5 cm) long
- 1 wooden dowel, ½ inch (1.3 cm) thick by 16 inches (41 cm) long
- thick cardboard
- string
- 1 cork, ½ inch (1.3 cm) wide
- paint and paintbrush
- stickers

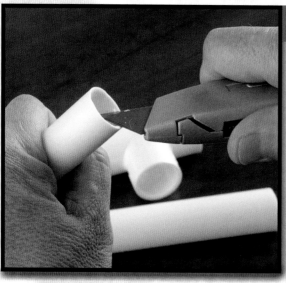

1

Ask an adult to help trim inside one end of the long pipe with a utility knife. The pipe end should be trimmed to a sharp edge. Trimming will help the cork fit in the end more easily.

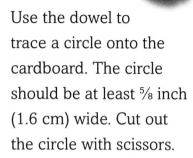

2

Use the dowel to trace a circle onto the cardboard. The circle should be at least ⅝ inch (1.6 cm) wide. Cut out the circle with scissors.

3

Use the screw to attach the cardboard circle to the end of the dowel. Be sure to screw it on through the center.

4

Measure 1½ inches (3.8 cm) from the same end of the dowel and make a mark with a pencil.

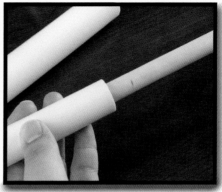

5 Slide the opposite end of the dowel through the sharpened end of the PVC pipe. Gently pull the cardboard circle through. Pull the dowel through the pipe until you see the pencil mark made in step 4.

6 Measure and mark 5 inches (13 cm) from the bare end of the dowel. Wrap electrical tape around the mark until it is too thick to fit into the pipe.

Cut a piece of string about 10 inches (25 cm) long. Tape one end to the tape roll on the dowel. Tape the other end to the close end of the pipe. Keep the string snug so the dowel doesn't come all the way out of the pipe.

7

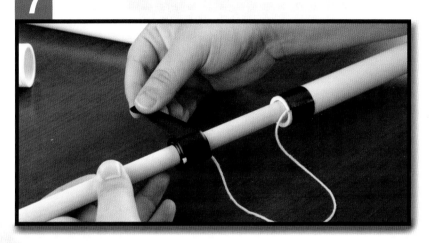

8

Wrap enough tape around the center of the long pipe so the T-connector will fit snugly.

Slide the T-connector onto the pipe and fit it around the tape. Then tape the ends of the connector in place.

Place the short pipe into the bottom of the connector. Tape in place to create the gun handle.

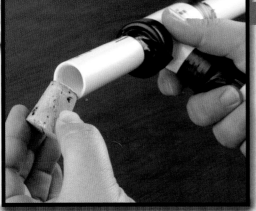

Place the cork in the open end of the gun barrel. If the cork is too large, ask an adult to trim the end of it with a utility knife. It should fit snugly into the pipe.

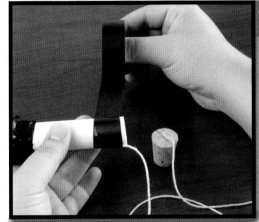

Cut a piece of string about 24 inches (60 cm) long. Staple one end of the string to the cork. Tape the other end to the gun barrel. Finally, paint and decorate the gun.

Hold the gun handle and push the dowel in. Watch your friends jump as the cork makes a loud pop and flies out of the gun barrel!

13

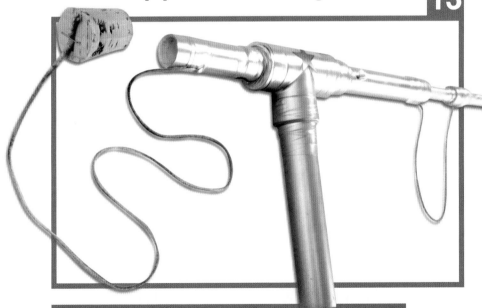

TIP

This toy gun isn't dangerous. But you should still be careful when using it. You should never shoot the cork at people, animals, or windows.

Farrell, Courtney. *Build It Green.* Let's Explore Science. Vero Beach, Fla.: Rourke Publishing LLC, 2010.

Popular Mechanics. *The Boy Mechanic: 200 Classic Things to Build.* New York: Hearst Books, 2006.

Strother, Scott. *The Adventurous Book of Outdoor Games: Classic Fun for Daring Boys and Girls.* Naperville, Ill.: Sourcebooks, 2008.

Internet Sites

FactHound offers a safe, fun way to find Internet sites related to this book. All of the sites on FactHound have been researched by our staff.

Here's all you do:

Visit *www.facthound.com*

Type in this code: 9781429654388

Check out projects, games and lots more at
www.capstonekids.com